Edinburgh Castle

Chris Tabraham
Principal Inspector of Ancient Monuments

'There are armed men and cannon in the citadel overhead; you may see the troops marshalled on the high parade; and at night after the early winter evenfall, and in the morning before the laggard winter dawn, the wind carries abroad over Edinburgh the sound of drums and bugles.'

(Robert Louis Stevenson,
Picturesque Old Edinburgh, *1878)*

21
23
22
9
18
19
CROWN SQUARE
20
17
WC
15
16
3
WC
2
LOWER WARD
1
ESPLANADE
Toilets
Castle Shop
Cafe/Restaurant

A Guided Tour

'The first and principall strength of the Realme.'

(KING JAMES VI, 1588)

MIDDLE WARD

Throughout the castle are twenty-six plaques drawing the visitor towards the most significant places of interest and giving 'at-a-glance' information. This guided tour follows that trail and reveals yet more of the castle's fascinating story. Please, never hesitate to ask one of our castle stewards if you wish to know more.

The tour begins at the Gatehouse [1] on the main east entry to the castle and passes through the Lower and Middle Wards to the summit of the rock - the Upper Ward - and Crown Square, the very heart of the castle. Then takes the visitor to places of interest slightly off the beaten track, ending at the Back Well [26] on the west side of the castle rock.

The Lower Ward

The eastern front of the castle, facing the town, was always the most vulnerable part and has suffered more siege damage than the rest of the defences. Its evolution was extremely complicated. Much of what stands today was built after the Lang (Long) Siege of 1571-3, and further improvements to the defences were made during the period of Jacobite disaffection in the early eighteenth century.

1 Gatehouse

Built in 1886-8 not as a true defensive building but as a conscious attempt to make the castle look more picturesque. The simple entrance gate that it replaced had been a more severely functional gate built in the later seventeenth century. Two seventeenth-century carved stone panels in the entrance passage show artillery, including the giant medieval siege gun, Mons Meg, which is still in the castle (see [21]). Bronze statues of King Robert the Bruce and Sir William Wallace were added on either side of the entrance in 1929.

The Dry Ditch fronting the Gatehouse dates to Cromwell's time in the 1650s. The Esplanade was created as a parade ground in 1753 and reached its present appearance by 1820.

2 Old Guardhouse & 3 Inner Barrier

Built in 1853 for the castle guard, the old guardhouse was extended in 1866 to accommodate a prison, and converted in 1989 to become the Castle Shop.

The inner barrier was built in the seventeenth century as a formidable obstacle between the outermost and inner gates. Originally fronted by a drawbridge and ditch, it has since been much altered.

4 PORTCULLIS GATE

The principal gateway into the castle following the great reconstruction ordered by Regent Morton after the Lang Siege of 1571-3. Raised on the ruins of the fourteenth-century Constable's Tower, it was a formidable obstacle with two outer doors, a portcullis and an inner door. The panel above the gateway is decorated with hearts and five-pointed stars (mullets) for James Douglas, fourth Earl of Morton, Regent under King James VI, and the builder of the Half-Moon Battery [16]. The armorial shield in the panel and the decorative upper works (the Argyle Tower [13]) were added in 1886-7.

The Middle Ward

In the Middle Ages the main part of the castle was on the summit of the rock - the Upper Ward. The Middle Ward was developed from the fifteenth century onwards for light industrial activities, like blacksmithing, and the present approach road was formed to aid the transport of heavy guns in and out of the castle.

5 Lang Stairs

A flight of 70 steps following the line of the principal medieval access to the summit, the Upper Ward. The curved wall a short way up on the right may be the stump of a tower from the medieval castle.

6 Argyle Battery

Also called the Six-Gun Battery. Together with the Mills Mount Battery (to its west) and the Low Defence (below it), this was the principal artillery defence on this north side of the castle. It was rebuilt in its present form in the 1730s on the recommendation of Major-General George Wade, best known for his military roads in the Scottish Highlands. The guns are cast-iron, muzzle-loading 18-pounders, made during the Napoleonic Wars of the early nineteenth century. Across the approach road from the Argyle Battery are the exposed foundations of the main guardhouse, built in 1801 but replaced in 1853 by the Old Guardhouse [2].

7 Cartshed

The only structure in the castle built in the immediate aftermath of the 1745-6 Jacobite Rising and now housing the visitor restaurant. Originally open-fronted, it was large enough to hold fifty carts for bringing provisions to the garrison from suppliers in the town. Archaeological excavations in this area in 1988-9 discovered the foundations of the seventeenth-century Storekeeper's House - demolished to make way for the Cartshed - as well as a rich assortment of structural remains and artefacts dating back to the late Bronze Age (about 900 BC). On Mills Mount Battery is the 'One o'clock Gun' (see page 46).

8 Governor's House

Built in 1742 as the official residence of the Castle Governor, with lodgings in the two wings for the Master Gunner and the Storekeeper. After the post of Governor was abolished in 1860 the building was used by the nursing sisters of the castle hospital. Today, the central block serves as the Army Officers' Mess with the north wing (on the right) reserved for the Governor, a Crown appointment restored for purely ceremonial purposes in 1935. **(No access for visitors)**

9 New Barracks

Built in 1796-9 to replace the outdated soldiers' barracks in the Great Hall [18] and providing enough accommodation for an infantry battalion (600 officers and men). It still serves a variety of military purposes. **(No access for visitors)**

Across the road from the New Barracks, in the Drill Hall of 1900, is the regimental museum of the Royal Scots.

The Upper Ward

Beyond Foog's Gate [10] is the Upper Ward, the highest part of the rock. This was the heart of the medieval castle, and very probably of the Dark-Age and Iron-Age forts which preceded it. The shape of the rock has been changed in several places by cutting away the basalt rock and elsewhere by building up to make a level base.

10 Foog's Gate

The origin of the name and the date of the structure are unknown. This was the main gate into the Upper Ward, in ancient times reached by the more difficult ascent up the Lang Stairs [5]. The perimeter wall on either side, part of the considerable defensive works built in King Charles II's reign (1649-85), was defended by gunholes and musketry loops. Inside, on the left, are two battlemented nineteenth-century water tanks and the former fire station, now the castle bookshop.

11 St Margaret's Chapel

The oldest structure surviving from the medieval castle. Built by King David I (1124-53) and dedicated to his mother, Saint Margaret, who died in the castle in 1093. A private oratory for the royal family, it passed out of use as a chapel in the sixteenth century and was converted into a gunpowder magazine. Its original purpose was rediscovered in 1845 and it was restored to its present condition.

This building, so plain outside, is a delight inside (see page 22). The space is divided into two by a fine arch decorated with chevron ornament. The semi-circular chancel at the east end housed the altar and was reserved for the priest officiating at the Mass. The rectangular nave was for the use of the élite congregation.

The chapel contains a copy of the Gospel Book owned by St Margaret. The stained-glass windows of St Andrew and St Ninian (in the chancel), St Columba, St Margaret and the national hero, Sir William Wallace, were designed by Douglas Strachan and installed in 1922.

12 Dog Cemetery

A little garden used since the 1840s as a burial place for officers' pet dogs and regimental mascots. The curved wall supporting the cemetery may survive from a tower of the medieval castle.

13 Argyle Tower

Named after Archibald, ninth Earl of Argyll, who is supposed to have been imprisoned in a chamber above the Portcullis Gate [4] before his execution in 1685. This top part of the Portcullis Gate is entirely the imaginative creation of Hippolyte Blanc, the Victorian architect who also restored the Great Hall [18]. Beneath is a vault which housed the mechanism for the sixteenth-century portcullis.

14 Forewall Battery & 15 Fore Well

Rebuilt in 1544 on the approximate line of the medieval defences, the Forewall Battery was heightened after the 1573 siege, and further reconstructed in the seventeenth century. Now armed with iron guns made about 1810 during the Napoleonic Wars.

The Fore Well was the main water supply for the Upper Ward from at least the early fourteenth century. It was almost 34 metres deep, but only the bottom 3 metres ever held water, giving a capacity of just 2,240 gallons (11,135 litres), barely capable of sustaining the garrison in times of siege. Augmented by the Back Well [26] in 1628, it finally went out of use in the nineteenth century and was replaced by a piped supply from the town.

16 Half-moon Battery

Built on the orders of Regent Morton after the Lang Siege of 1571-3 as the principal high-level battery on the castle's most vulnerable eastern front. The gun battery was damaged in the sieges of 1650 and 1689 and repaired much as it appears now. The two iron fire-baskets were used to give alarm in an emergency. The guns are replica 18-pounders of the early nineteenth century. Until the eighteenth century, the battery was armed with the 'Seven Sisters', bronze guns made in the castle in the early sixteenth century.

The Buildings in Crown Square

Crown Square was created in the fifteenth century as the principal courtyard of the castle. The platform on which it stands is artificial, formed by a series of great stone vaults (see [21]) built on the south-facing slopes of the castle rock. The name 'Crown Square' came into use after the discovery of the Scottish Crown and the other regalia in the Palace [17] in 1818; before that time it was known as Palace Yard.

17 Royal Palace

The residence in the castle of the later Stewart kings and queens. As you see it today it is the result of a long succession of alterations and additions. It reached its peak of importance in the reign of Mary Queen of Scots (1542-67). She gave birth here to the future King James VI (and I of England) on 19 June 1566, in the tiny room opening off the chamber now known as Queen Mary's Room. The exterior and interior of the Palace were greatly remodelled for King James VI's 'hamecoming' in 1617 (see page 34). The Crown Room on the first floor still houses the Honours of Scotland, the most ancient regalia surviving in the United Kingdom (see page 36). Beside them is the Stone of Destiny, returned to Scotland from Westminster Abbey, London, in 1996.

18 Great Hall

Built before King James IV's death in 1513 as the chief place of great ceremony and State assembly in the castle. Converted into a soldiers' barracks during Cromwell's occupation in the 1650s and further altered in 1737 to house 312 men. Following the building of the New Barracks [9] about 1800, it became a hospital until 1887. It was then somewhat fancifully 'restored' by the architect Hippolyte Blanc (see [13]), who was responsible for almost everything you see except the original great hammer-beam roof supported on projecting stone corbels - one of the most important timber roofs in Scotland. The ends of the hammer-beams have carved human and animal masks, and there is a design on each of the corbels, including: IR4 crowned as the cipher of King James (Iacobus Rex) the Fourth; the crowned royal arms; Scottish thistles; fleurs-de-lys to symbolise the 'auld alliance' with France; and vases containing both thistles and roses to symbolise the new English connection with the marriage between King James IV and Margaret Tudor in 1503. (The arms of Governors of the castle painted on the terminals of the secondary rafters date from the restoration by Blanc.)

(19) Queen Anne Building

In the later Middle Ages, this area seems to have been occupied by the kitchens serving the Great Hall [18] together with the House of the Artillery or the Gunhouse, and may have been Mons Meg's first home in Edinburgh Castle. The present building was inspired by the French invasion scare of 1708 and provided accommodation for staff officers, including the barrack master, master gunner, school master and chaplain. It was remodelled in 1933 as the Naval and Military Museum to complement the newly-opened Scottish National War Memorial [20] and is currently undergoing repair.

(20) Scottish National War Memorial

St Mary's Church stood on this site in the Middle Ages, but this was converted into a munition house in 1540 and demolished in 1755 to make room for a new barracks. This North Barracks, improved by Robert Billings in 1863 to give it a more picturesque appearance, was vacated by the Army in 1923 and was adapted by Sir Robert Lorimer as the National Shrine.

On 14 July, 1927 the Prince of Wales (later King Edward VIII) opened this memorial to the Scottish dead of the 1914-18 Great War. The building now also commemorates those who fell in the Second World War and in medal areas since 1945.

The exterior of the Memorial is enriched with symbolic sculpture - the animals in the windows and niches representing the Vices and Virtues; the humans on the Crown Square elevation signifying Courage (mailed figure with sword and shield), Peace (a female with doves), Justice (blindfolded with scales and a sword), and Mercy (a warrior with a child). Above the door the figure rising from a phoenix denotes the survival of the Spirit.

Within is the Hall of Honour - or the Hall of the Regiments as it was first called - and beyond it an apse containing the Shrine, wherein lies the steel casket containing a complete Roll of Honour of the Scottish dead. The figure of St Michael the Archangel soars above. The stained-glass windows by Douglas Strachan and the bronze friezes by Alice and Morris Meredith-Williams give vivid impressions of the Great War.

Off the Beaten Track

For visitors with time to explore further, a visit to other places of interest, slightly off the beaten track, is recommended. These are situated below and to the west of the Upper Ward. Much of the western part of the rock was not developed until the early seventeenth century.

21 Castle Vaults

Built in the fifteenth century directly onto the uneven rock to form a level surface - now Crown Square - above. Through their history the Vaults have had a variety of uses - as stores, as part of the arsenal, as soldiers' barracks, as bakehouse, as civil and military prison as well as a prison of war (see page 40). One of the Vaults now houses the giant medieval siege gun, Mons Meg (see page 27).

22 Military Prison & 23 Dury's Battery

The prison was built about 1842 for soldiers from the castle garrison and extended in the 1880s. Last used in 1923, when the garrison moved to Redford Barracks in the Edinburgh suburbs. This little military prison was a miniature version of the great civilian prisons of the day, such as Perth, with an open hall giving access to two floors of cells.

Dury's Battery was the main south-facing battery, named after Captain Theodore Dury, military engineer for Scotland, who built it between 1708 and 1713. Dury also designed the Queen Anne Building [19]. The guns are iron 18-pounders made about 1810.

24 Ordnance Storehouse & 25 Hospital

Two stores for arms and military equipment were built on either side of a courtyard to a design by William Skinner in 1753. Skinner, as a military engineer, is best known for his magnificent Highland fortress at Fort George, near Inverness (also in Historic Scotland's care and open to visitors). The main gunpowder magazine originally stood on the west side of the same courtyard. This was demolished in 1897 and the two storehouses then redesigned as a military hospital, formerly house in the Great Hall [18]. The north ordnance storehouse is now the headquarters of the Scottish United Services Museum.

From the viewpoint on the west side of Hospital Square can be seen the castle's Western Defences. This is an exposed, and hazardous, part of the castle - an historic problem for in 1677 a report noted that the sentries on patrol found it impossible to go along it 'in a stormy night'. In King Charles II's reign (1649-85) a defensive wall was rebuilt and a walkway provided along the western edge of the rock for patrolling guards. It was at the sallyport (back gate) through this wall, on 19 March 1689, that Viscount Dundee conferred with the Governor, the Duke of Gordon. After the meeting, 'Bonnie' Dundee rode north to raise a force to support King James VII and the Governor began his defence of the castle on behalf of the exiled monarch. During the 1715 siege, the Jacobites tried to breach the sallyport. This prompted Major-General Wade to propose that the Western Defences be redesigned. The work was carried out by William Adam, the famous architect, working in his capacity as a building contractor. The walls were designed for defence by musketeers. The uppermost terrace (immediately below the viewpoint) was constructed in 1858.

26 Back Well

Cut out of the basalt in 1628 to improve the castle's water supply (see [15]). A mere 2.5 metres deep, it was more a cistern than a well, collecting water draining off the rock.

Beyond the Back Well and inside the New Barracks is the regimental museum of the Royal Scots Dragoon Guards.

Edinburgh Castle Symbol of Scotland

The volcanic castle rock in Edinburgh was born over 340 million years ago following a violent eruption deep in the earth's crust. Its story as a place of human habitation stretches back a mere 3,000 years, to the late Bronze Age. It was evidently a thriving hill-top settlement when Roman soldiers marched by in the first century AD. And the first mention of Din Eidyn, 'the stronghold of Eidyn', comes shortly before AD 600 when in the hall on the top of the rock the war-band of the local king, Mynyddog, pledged themselves to die in the service of their lord.

The place had become an important royal fortress by the time of Queen Margaret's death there in November 1093. Throughout the Middle Ages Edinburgh Castle ranked as one of the major castles of the kingdom and its story is very much the story of Scotland. But with the building of the Palace of Holyroodhouse in the early sixteenth century, the castle was used less and less as a royal residence, though it remained symbolically the heart of the kingdom.

The castle increasingly became the centre of the military arm of government. Almost all the medieval buildings were either converted to military use or demolished; the old medieval defences were replaced by new artillery fortifications. The castle was last besieged during the 1745-6 Jacobite Rising.

Since that time, this mighty fortress has become a powerful national symbol of Scotland.

The castle rock, painted in 1811 by Francis Towne.
(Courtesy of Christie's.)

The Castle Rock

The castle rock and the Royal Mile are perhaps the world's best example of the geological feature known as a 'crag-and-tail'. Its origin goes back about 340 million years. Hot molten rock rose though the earth's crust and spread ash and lavas over the landscape to form a huge cone-shaped volcano. In time the volcano became extinct. Millions of years later great sheets of ice came and eroded the soft sedimentary rocks that had by this time covered the volcano. The last Ice Age, some ten to twenty thousand years ago, was so powerful that it removed almost everything but the volcano's solid basalt feeder pipe. The ice, moving from west to east, flowed around the obstacle and gouged out the areas now known as Princes Street Gardens and The Grassmarket. But the hard basalt protected the softer sediments to its east, and by the time the streams of ice merged once more near the site of Holyrood Palace, the 'crag-and-tail' - the castle rock and Edinburgh's Royal Mile - had been created.

A Prehistoric Fort

Man may first have stood on the castle rock about eight thousand years ago when Stone-Age hunters and gatherers appeared in the densely-wooded and boggy landscape. Recent archaeological excavations in the area of the Cartshed [7] have discovered evidence for a settlement of round houses on the rock dating to the late Bronze Age (about 900 BC). After a period of greatly reduced activity, the hill-top settlement blossomed again during the first and second centuries AD, by which date the Roman Empire had established its most northerly frontier, the Antonine Wall (built in AD 142-3), a little to the west of Edinburgh. The archaeologists found a wealth of Roman material, suggesting close contact between the native Votadini tribe and the Roman military in the region.

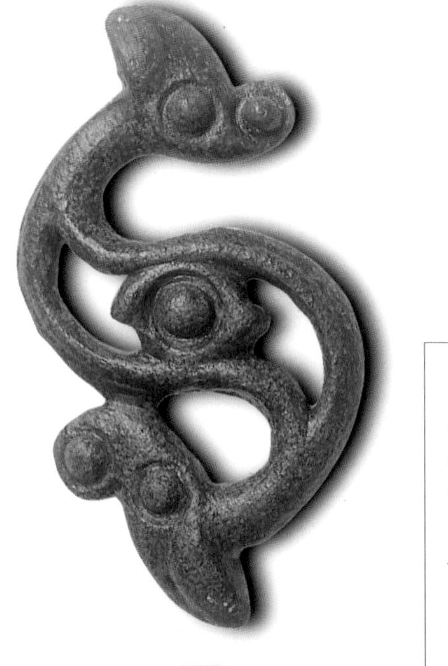

An impression of daily life in the prehistoric fort about AD 100, using information from the recent excavations in the area of the Cartshed [7]. The two bronze brooches date from the same period.

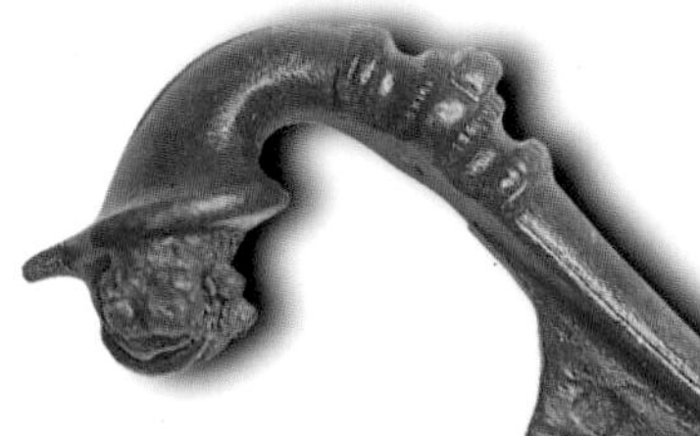

Din Eidyn

In time the Votadini tribe came to be known as the Gododdin, and it is with the Gododdin that the castle rock first appears on record shortly before AD 600. The war-band of the Gododdin was gathered with their king, Mynyddog Mwynfawr, in Din Eidyn, 'the stronghold of Eidyn'. In the taper-lit hall the 300 men with the bard Aneirin pledged themselves in drink to die in the service of their lord.

And all but a few did die, on a raid into the territories of the Angles in about AD 600, at Catraeth (Catterick in Yorkshire). Retreating to their tribal lands, the Gododdin were pursued by the Angles. Din Eidyn was besieged and taken in 638, and the place seems then to have received the English name - Edinburgh - which it has kept ever since.

This bone comb, found in the recent archaeological excavations, is probably of eighth-century date.

A Royal Castle

In 1018 King Malcolm II defeated the English at the Battle of Carham and firmly secured for Scotland the territory between the Firth of Forth and the River Tweed. A royal castle at Edinburgh first emerges at the end of that century.

On 16 November 1093 Queen Margaret, seriously ill in Edinburgh Castle, returned to her chamber from Mass to be told of the killing of her husband, King Malcolm III, by the English at the Battle of Alnwick. The news caused her death and her body was taken out of the castle through the western postern gate and buried in Dunfermline Abbey in Fife.

By the time of the reign of Malcolm and Margaret's youngest son, King David I (1124-53), the rocky summit was a thriving royal castle, serving as a royal residence, as a storehouse, as the headquarters of the sheriff (the king's administrative officer for his shire of Edinburgh), and as a prison. David was probably responsible for the earliest surviving building on the castle rock, the little Romanesque chapel [11] later dedicated to his mother, who was canonised as St Margaret in 1250.

Outside the castle, Edinburgh already existed as a royal burgh in King David's reign. It was an important burgh, but not the most important or the largest in Scotland. Only by the reign of King James III (1460-88) could it be called the capital of the country.

The interior of St Margaret's Chapel looking east towards the fine Romanesque chancel arch and apse.

Robert the Bruce and the Wars with England

King Robert the Bruce's statue on the east front of the Gatehouse [1]. The silver coin (right), minted in England during Edward II's reign (1307-27) and found at the castle during the recent excavations, is tangible proof of the English occupation.

With the exception of St Margaret's Chapel, nothing survives of the early royal castle. We have King Robert I (the Bruce) to thank for that!

In 1296 King Edward I of England invaded Scotland and Edinburgh Castle soon fell into his hands. A large garrison was installed - 347 strong in 1300. After the English king's death in 1307, the English grasp on Scotland weakened. In the spring of 1314, a surprise night attack led by Sir Thomas Randolph, Earl of Moray and Bruce's nephew, recaptured the castle. It was a daring plan that won the place, involving a party of thirty hand-picked men making the very difficult ascent up the north precipice and taking the garrison by surprise. Bruce immediately ordered the dismantling of the defences to prevent reoccupation by the English. Shortly after, Bruce's army routed the English at the Battle of Bannockburn, near Stirling.

After Bruce's death in 1329, hostilities again broke out and in 1335 the castle once more fell into English hands. Major repairs were carried out but these proved ineffective against another storybook assault in April 1341, this time led by Sir William Douglas. Douglas's party, disguised as merchants bringing supplies to the garrison, managed to drop its loads at the castle gates, so preventing their closure. A larger force hidden nearby rushed to join them and the castle was taken. Most of the English garrison had their throats cut or their heads chopped off and their bodies thrown over the crags.

The Saint Margaret window in the tiny chapel that bears her name.

David's Tower

In 1356 King David II, Robert the Bruce's son, returned to Scotland from a 10-year captivity in England. He straightaway set about rebuilding his castle at Edinburgh.

King David II (left) greets King Edward III of England about 1350. (COURTESY OF THE BRITISH LIBRARY.)

The first task was the rebuilding of St Mary's Church (which stood on the site of the Scottish National War Memorial [20]) which had been converted into a granary during the English occupation. In 1361 a new well was sunk at the base of the north face of the rock, by which route the castle had been taken in 1314, and the Well-House Tower, now visible in West Princes Street Gardens, was built beside it to defend this tortuous approach.

In 1368 work began on a massive L-shaped tower house crowning the eastern crags. The tower, subsequently named David's Tower, was intended as a secure royal lodging as well as the main defence towards the burgh. It was extensively battered by cannon during the Lang Siege of 1571-3 and it survives only as a ruin, entombed within the Half-Moon Battery which replaced it as the chief defence on the eastern side of the castle.

David's Tower was monumentally impressive. It stood over 30 m high and comprised three floors of accommodation - a ground-floor vault that may have served as a strongroom of the Treasury; a first-floor hall, or private reception room; and a second-floor private apartment, including the king's bedchamber. Only a part of the ground floor and a stretch of stone curtain wall to its south remain.

King David died in 1371 without seeing his great tower completed. It was left to his successor King Robert II, the first Stewart monarch, to continue the rebuilding work. In 1433 work began on a new Great Chamber for King James I. This building, intended to complement the restricted accommodation within David's Tower, may still remain, albeit greatly altered, in the two seventeenth-century rooms in the present Palace now called the Laich Hall and Chamber.

The 'Black Dinner' of 1440

King James II as a young man.
(Courtesy of the Württemberg State Library.)

It was either in the Great Chamber or in the hall in David's Tower that one of the most dastardly episodes in the castle's history took place - the 'Black Dinner' of 1440.

King James II had succeeded his murdered father, King James I, in 1437. Just a young lad, he was in the care of Sir William Crichton, Keeper of Edinburgh Castle and arch-rival of the Douglases. Crichton soon used his powerful position in a spectacular political assassination.

Crichton invited the sixth Earl of Douglas, a teenager himself, and his younger brother to dine with the king in the castle. The two guests were greeted 'with great joy and gladness' at the castle gates. They 'banqueted royally with all delicacies that could be got (and) after great cheer was made at the dinner and the courses taken away (Crichton) presented a bull's head before the earl which was a sign and token of condemnation to death'. The young king protested at this outrage but to no effect. The Douglases were taken to an adjacent chamber, summarily tried on a trumped-up charge of treason and beheaded in the castle courtyard.

The main door into David's Tower and (right) an English spy's drawing of the castle in 1544. David's Tower is shown standing to its full height, dominating all else.

Mons Meg (left) with other guns and military equipment is depicted on a 17th-century stone panel visible in the entrance passage of the Gatehouse [1].

Mons Meg

In 1457 King James II, now ruling in person, was given a present of two giant siege guns (called 'bombards') by his uncle-by-marriage, Philip the Good, Duke of Burgundy. One of the guns survives and is on display in the Castle Vaults [21]. This is Mons Meg.

Mons Meg - or 'Mons' as she was then simply known - was made at Mons (in present-day Belgium) in 1449. It was at the leading edge of artillery technology at the time: a muzzle-loaded piece weighing over 6 tons (6040 kg) and firing gunstones weighing 330 lbs (150 kg). It soon saw action against the English and was taken to the siege of Norham Castle, on the River Tweed, in 1497. But its great weight made it ponderously slow to drag around - it could only make about 3 miles (5 km) a day - and by the middle of the sixteenth century it was retired from military service and restricted to firing salutes from the castle ramparts. In 1558 Mons was fired to celebrate the marriage of Mary Queen of Scots to the French Dauphin, Francis. The gunstone fired that day was recovered from Wardie Muir - almost 2 miles (3.5 km) away!

When Mons Meg was last fired, on 14 October 1681 in a birthday salute for the Duke of Albany and York (later King James VII and II), its barrel burst, fracturing two hoops. The ancient bombard was unceremoniously dumped beside Foog's Gate [10] where it lay until 1754 when it was taken south to the Tower of London. Mons Meg was returned to the castle in 1829 (see page 42).

A Renaissance Palace

The Palace in Crown Square, the royal residence in the castle. King Charles I was the last monarch to reside here the night before his coronation in 1633.

King James IV, from a tableau in the 'Honours of the Kingdom' exhibition in the first floor of the Palace.

During the reign of King James III (1460-88), Edinburgh finally emerged as the capital city. About this time the castle was replanned. The focal point was a new courtyard, the quadrangle for long called Palace Yard and now Crown Square, around which was placed the principal royal accommodation.

The creation of Crown Square was a huge task involving the construction of massive stone vaults over the whole of the basalt rock platform sloping southwards from St Mary's Church. As well as providing a level platform for Crown Square, the Castle Vaults [21] provided ample room for stores.

The Palace [17] and St Mary's Church (see [20]) already stood along the east and north sides of the new courtyard. Along the west side was placed the Gunhouse, where the royal artillery was displayed. This was probably Mons Meg's first home in the castle. The south side was occupied by the Great Hall [18], the principal banqueting and reception room. This greatly restored but still impressive building was probably completed late in the reign of King James IV (1488-1513).

By the time of King James' death, on the bloody battlefield of Flodden, Edinburgh Castle was the principal royal castle in the realm. It was a formidable fortress, a royal palace, the chief arsenal, a treasury for the crown jewels, the repository of the national archives, the residence of several officers of state including the Treasurer, and a state prison. As a prison it was not entirely escape-proof as Alexander, the Duke of Albany and King James III's brother, proved in 1479. After killing his guards Albany lowered himself down the rock on a rope tied to his window. His companion slipped and injured himself, but Albany carried him to the port of Leith and freedom.

King James IV's monogram - IR4 (Jacobus Rex IV) - on one of the stone corbels supporting the great roof.

The impressive Great Hall with its splendid medieval hammerbeam roof.

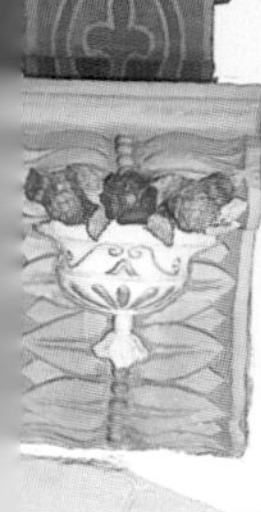

thistles flank ngle red rose stone corbel, bolising the riage in 1503 ing James IV Margaret or of England.

The stone corbels supporting the roof, with their remarkable carvings, are probably the earliest Renaissance architectural ornament in Scotland.

Queen Mary and the Birth of Prince James

The castle on the rock was never the most comfortable or healthy of royal residences. In the thirteenth century, King Alexander III's young queen, Margaret, described it as a 'sad and solitary place, without greenery and, because of its nearness to the sea, unwholesome' (a reference to the thick sea-mist, or haar, which still envelops the castle from time to time). Nevertheless, it was the foremost castle of the land and in 1566 was chosen as the place where Mary Queen of Scots should give birth to her first and only child. Queen Mary had married her second husband, her cousin Henry Stewart, Lord Darnley, in July 1565 and was expecting their child in June 1566.

Mary Queen of Scots (Courtesy of the National Galleries of Scotland).

The Queen took up residence in the Palace [17] in April. Her lodging comprised the Great Chamber built in 1433, a large Inner Chamber, which was both reception room and bedroom, and an innermost small private room called the Cabinet. It was in the Cabinet on the morning of Wednesday 19 June that Queen Mary gave birth to a baby prince, James. The infant, who in time would unite the Crowns of Scotland and England as King James VI of Scotland and I of England, was taken from the Cabinet to the Inner Chamber and displayed to representatives of a thankful nation.

The stone (right) with the date 1566 and the monogram MAH (for Mary and Henry, Lord Darnley) is above the elaborate round-headed door leading from Crown Square to the royal lodging in the Palace (see the photograph on the preceding page).

The Cabinet in the Palace where Prince James was born in 1566. The painted decoration was added in preparation for King James VI's 'hamecoming' in 1617, and the lower panelling was added in 1848 shortly after the room was first opened to visitors.

The Lang Siege of 1571-3

The assault on the castle, May 1573, from Holinshed's Chronicles.

On 6 May 1567, Mary Queen of Scots returned to the castle with James Hepburn, Earl of Bothwell, in her retinue: the artillery 'schot maist magnificentlie' to welcome her. Nine days later, she and Bothwell were married. The union provoked a large section of the nobility to rebel. Queen Mary surrendered at the Battle of Carberry Hill in June, and was imprisoned in Lochleven Castle where she was forced to abdicate in favour of her son. Escaping ten months later, she fought and lost her last battle at Langside, near Glasgow, before fleeing to England.

Despite her departure, there were still those in Scotland who continued to support the queen's cause. Amongst them was Sir William Kirkcaldy of Grange, Keeper of Edinburgh Castle. By the summer of 1571 he was defiantly holding the fortress against the Regent governing on behalf of the infant King James. A

for well over a year (hence its name - the Lang Siege) until in 1573 Regent Morton sought help from Queen Elizabeth I of England. An English agent reported that 'there is no mining that can prevail in this rock but only battery with ordnance to beat down the walls'.

Heavy guns were duly despatched by sea from Berwick and six batteries were set up outside the castle. Within ten days of the massive bombardment opening up on 16 May, much of the east side of the castle had been reduced to rubble, including most of David's Tower, the Constable's Tower and the stretch of wall in between. The east elevation of the Palace, where King James VI had been born just seven years earlier, was badly damaged and its three fine oriel windows largely destroyed. With the main water-supply - the Fore Well [15] - choked by the collapse of David's Tower, Kirkcaldy of Grange had no option other than to surrender.

An impression of the building of the Half-Moon Battery and Portcullis Gate following the Lang Siege.

The Castle Rebuilt

The panel above the Portcullis Gate is decorated with hearts and mullets (stars), the armorial insignia of Regent Morton.

Work was immediately put in hand to re construct the castle after the Lang Siege. Much of the effort went into securing the defences of 'the first and principal strength of the realm' but scant attention was given to the residential accommodation. After this the monarch's Edinburgh residence was at Holyrood Palace.

The most significant task was the building of a great defence, the Half-Moon Battery [16], around the ruined stump of David's Tower, which was now buried from view. The rounded shape of the battery enabled its numerous guns to provide a wide horizontal sweep of fire. This firepower was augmented by guns emplaced on the rebuilt Forewall Battery [14] which ran northward from the Half-Moon Battery to a new portcullised gate-tower - the Portcullis Gate [4] - built to replace the Constable's Tower.

James Douglas, fourth Earl of Morton and Regent of Scotland, was responsible for the rebuilding of the castle following the Lang Siege. (COURTESY OF THE NATIONAL GALLERIES OF SCOTLAND.)

The Portcullis Gate.

King James VI's 'Hamecoming' of 1617

The Laich Hall, restored in 1998.

King James VI and I of England, painted by Paul van Somer about the time of the monarch's return to his native land.
(Courtesy of the Royal Collection © Her Majesty The Queen.)

In 1603 Queen Elizabeth of England died unmarried and without children. Her heir was King James VI of Scotland, descended from Elizabeth's grandfather through the marriage between King James IV and Margaret Tudor. King James VI and his queen, Anne of Denmark, soon headed south for London. The king returned only once, in 1617.

In advance of the royal 'hamecoming', works were carried out to prepare the castle for the king's visit. The most important task was the refurbishment of the Palace [17] which had received such a battering during the Lang Siege. Much of what the visitor sees today is the result of this operation.

Inside the Palace the fourteenth-century Great Chamber was divided into two rooms, now called the Laich Hall and Chamber, while two new floors above provided royal lodgings for King James and Queen Anne (although in the event she chose not to accompany her husband in 1617). The ornate interior decorations - the plaster ceilings, the wood panelling, the painting work - provided for the king's delight have long since gone; all except the decoration in the little Cabinet where His Majesty was born.

The centrepiece in the decoration of King James' birthplace was this large representation of the royal arms of Scotland above the inscription:

Lord Jesu Chryst that Crounit was with Thornse
Preserve the Birth quhais Badgie heir is borne
And send Hir Sonee Successione to Reigne still
Lang in this Realme, if that it be Thy will
Als grant O Lord quhat ever of Hir proseed
Be to Thy Glorie Honer and Prais sobied.

The show-piece of the refurbished Palace externally was the east front facing the Old Town. Unlike the other sides, which were of rubble masonry, this side was built of fine ashlar. The wall-top was attractively finished with a cannon-studded battlemented parapet and square turrets with ogee-shaped lead roofs. The windows had stone mullions and transoms protected by iron cage grilles. Above them were ornamented pediments containing royal emblems, including the Crown, the monogram IR6 (for Jacobus Rex 6), the date 1616 and swags of fruit. Of the two richly carved frames between the upper windows, one encloses a panel showing the Honours of Scotland; the other is now blank but it originally held the royal arms of Scotland.

The CROWN in its present form was made for King James V in 1540 by the Edinburgh goldsmith, John Mosman, who lived on the site in Edinburgh's Royal Mile where the John Knox House stands today. He melted down the gold from the previous Crown, added more gold brought from Upper Clydesdale and increased the number of gemstones. The Crown was first worn by King James V at the coronation of his second queen, Mary of Guise, in 1540.

The SWORD was presented to King James IV by Pope Julius II in 1507. It was accompanied by a scabbard and belt, and all three pieces are outstanding examples of Italian Renaissance craftsmanship. Their creator was Domenico da Sutri.

The Honours of Scotland

The refurbishment of the Palace in 1615-17 included the provision of a strongroom to house the Honours of Scotland, the 'Crown Jewels'. The Crown Room, situated on the first floor, still houses the Honours, the oldest regalia in the United Kingdom and amongst the oldest surviving in Christendom.

The Honours of Scotland - the Crown, Sword and Sceptre - were shaped in Italy and Scotland during the reigns of King James IV and King James V and were first used together as coronation regalia at the enthronement of the infant Queen Mary in Stirling Castle in September 1543. From the time they were taken from Edinburgh Castle in 1650 to be used at the coronation of King Charles II at Scone on New Year's Day 1651, they have had an eventful history. Between 1651 and 1660 they were preserved from capture by Cromwell's army, at first in Dunnottar Castle on the Kincardineshire coast and then, with Dunnottar besieged, smuggled out by the wife of the minister of nearby Kinneff Church, and buried under the church floor.

After the 1707 Treaty of Union between Scotland and England, the Honours were locked away in the Crown Room and the doors walled up. 111 years later, Walter Scott, with the permission of the Prince Regent (the future King George IV), had the room unblocked and the chest forced open. The Honours were rediscovered and immediately displayed to the public. They have remained on display ever since, except for a period during the Second World War when they were buried once again, this time in David's Tower.

The SCEPTRE was presented to King James IV, probably in 1494 by Pope Alexander VI. It was remodelled for King James V in 1536 by the Edinburgh silversmith Andrew Leys. He lengthened the rod and embellished the finial.

A Garrison Fortress

King James VI was a reluctant visitor to Edinburgh Castle, much preferring the more amenable surroundings of Holyrood Palace. King Charles I was similarly inclined, visiting the castle only once, the night before his coronation as King of Scots in 1633 - the last occasion a reigning monarch slept in the castle.

The 79th Highlanders march out through Foog's Gate in 1853, painted by R R McIan. (COURTESY OF THE QUEEN'S OWN HIGHLANDERS REGIMENTAL MUSEUM.)

King Charles' execution, and the unequivocal Scottish support for his rightful successor, King Charles II, brought Oliver Cromwell to Scotland. By Christmas Day 1650 the English 'Roundheads' had set up their headquarters in Edinburgh Castle and their presence was to have a profound effect on the fortress. Among the works undertaken by them were a new eastern defence - the Dry Ditch fronting the Gatehouse [1] - and the conversion of the Great Hall [18] into a soldiers' barrack.

But it was Cromwell's creation of a permanent standing army - his New Model Army - that was to transform the ancient royal castle into a garrison fortress. Before Cromwell's time the Scottish army - the 'host' - had been called into the field only when occasion demanded. Lords and lieges, cottars and tenants left their homes and loved ones to fight for their country, and the castle was 'stuffed with men' only in times of crisis. When King Charles returned to his throne in 1660 he continued the idea of a regular, paid army, and from then until after the First World War. a permanent garrison of soldiers was stationed in the castle.

During that time the medieval castle was transformed into a garrison fortress, and much of what the visitor sees today dates from this phase of use. Some important medieval buildings were demolished: St Mary's Church went in 1755 to be replaced by the North Barracks (now the Scottish National War Memorial [20]); the Gunhouse in 1708 to be replaced by an officers' barrack (the Queen Anne Building [19]). Almost every available space was given over to Army use, including the royal apartments in the Palace [17]. Even King James VI's birth-chamber was pressed into military use. The only room not requisitioned by the Army was the Crown Room in the Palace, the repository of the Honours of Scotland. New buildings were erected, amongst them the Governor's House [8] in 1742, the Ordnance Storehouses [24 & 25] in 1755, the New Barracks [9] in the 1790s and the Military Prison [22] in 1842.

The defences too were greatly transformed, for the castle was still subject to attack. In 1689 the Duke of Gordon unsuccessfully defended the castle for the exiled King James VII against the forces of William and Mary, and the skeletons of 15 well-built men recently discovered beside the Old Guardhouse [2] could well have been soldiers serving in the garrison at that time. During the 1715 Rising the Jacobites actually broke through the sallyport at the Western Defences, an event which prompted the military authorities to undertake major works. Throughout the 1720s and '30s most of the artillery defences now seen protecting the castle on its north and west sides were built. They were soon put to the test during the 1745 Jacobite Rising, but only in a desultory fashion. Bonnie Prince Charlie's half-hearted effort to take the fortress proved to be the last military action the castle saw.

zig-zag artillery fortifications
g the north side of the castle, and
and the Western Defences (inset),
mainly from the 1730s. They were
t on the advice of Major-General
rge Wade, Commander-in-Chief
cotland, and designed by Captain
a Romer. The work was carried
by William Adam, the noted
itect, working in his capacity
uilding contractor to the Board
rdnance.

The French Prisons

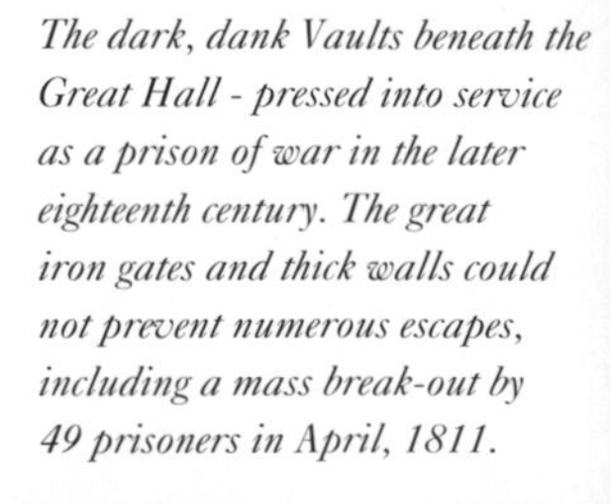

The dark, dank Vaults beneath the Great Hall - pressed into service as a prison of war in the later eighteenth century. The great iron gates and thick walls could not prevent numerous escapes, including a mass break-out by 49 prisoners in April, 1811.

Many of the Jacobite prisoners taken in the '45 Rising were confined in the castle. They included the Earl of Kellie, MacDonell of Glengarry and MacDonald of Glencoe. Jacobite suspects were still being brought there as late as 1753.

It was during the Seven Years' War (1757-63) that the best-remembered use of the castle as a prison of war began. In April 1757 the crew of a French privateer were brought to the castle; they were soon followed by others, and by the end of the war there were 500 Frenchmen, mostly sailors, incarcerated in the Castle Vaults [21] beneath the Great Hall. The Vaults were pressed into service as prisons of war once again during the War of American Independence (1775-83), though this time several nationalities - not only Americans, but French, Spanish, Dutch and Irish - were represented.

The wars with Revolutionary and Napoleonic France (1793-1815) saw the climax of the castle's use as prison of war. Again most of the captives were sailors, but soldiers later arrived from Wellington's victories in Spain. They were a mixed bag - Frenchmen, Spaniards, Dutch, Germans, Italians and Americans - and in the crowded, squalid conditions feuds developed between the various nationalities. However, between arguments the prisoners used their time and talents to make articles which they were permitted to sell to visitors; the more enterprising amongst them forged banknotes.

The prisoners of war left their mark in the Vaults - on the stonework (above) and on the woodwork (below: 'LORD NORD' - Lord North, the British Prime Minister - dangling from a hangman's gallows with the date 1780; and (bottom) a ship flying the American flag from its stern).

Assorted bone dies made and used by the prisoners for forging banknotes (By permission of The Governor and Company of the Bank of Scotland © 1994)

A Public Attraction

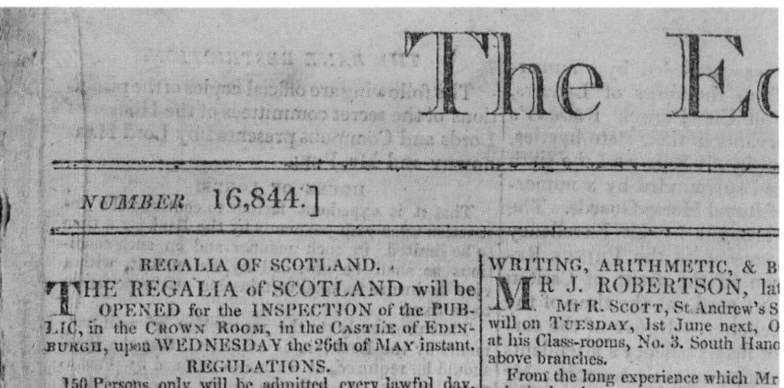

The Ed

NUMBER 16,844.]

REGALIA OF SCOTLAND.

THE REGALIA of SCOTLAND will be OPENED for the INSPECTION of the PUBLIC, in the CROWN ROOM, in the CASTLE of EDINBURGH, upon WEDNESDAY the 26th of MAY instant.

REGULATIONS.

150 Persons only will be admitted every lawful day. The hours of admission betwixt ten and three o'clock.

Orders will be issued at the shop of ROBERT CAMERON, jun. and Co. stationers, No. 2. Bank Street, upon payment of One Shilling for each person; commencing on the day of opening.

To prevent mistakes, applications for orders (by persons not calling themselves) to be made *in writing*, to R. C. jun. & Co. as above, specifying the names of the persons for whom the orders are wished.

EDINBURGH CASTLE, 20th May 1819.

WRITING, ARITHMETIC, & B

MR J. ROBERTSON, lat
. MR R. SCOTT, St Andrew's S
will on TUESDAY, 1st June next, O
at his Class-rooms, No. 3. South Hano
above branches.

From the long experience which Mr
principal assistant to Mr Scott for these
in teaching the above branches of educ
public school, as well as in families an
he trusts that he will be able to do just
who may be intrusted to his care.

The most approved modern style in w
in book-keeping and arithmetic, will b

The class-rooms are large, well aired
easy access, and in a very centrical part

N. B.—Private teaching, as usual
boarding schools.

One chilly morning in February 1818, Walter Scott, the famous novelist, together with the Governor of the castle and other officers of State, watched as the door of the Crown Room was broken down and the locks of the great oak chest they found inside burst open. Their quest was for the ancient Honours of Scotland and they were overjoyed at finding them exactly as they had been left after the Treaty of Union with England 111 years earlier.

An advertisement (above) in the EDINBURGH EVENING COURANT, 24 May 1819, invites visitors (right) to view the newly found Honours of Scotland for the princely sum of one shilling (about £7.50).

The Honours were almost immediately placed on public display and amongst the first to visit the Crown Room was King George IV, who as Prince Regent had granted the Royal Warrant permitting Scott to search for them. King George did so as part of a triumphal visit to Scotland in 1822, the first by a reigning monarch since King Charles II's in 1651. The Honours of Scotland were taken down to Holyrood Palace for the duration of the king's stay and the highlight of the visit was His Majesty's procession to the castle to return the Honours to the Crown Room.

The rediscovery of the Honours and their placing on public display heralded a new and enduring use for the castle - as a visitor attraction. People flocked to the castle just to view the ancient regalia, paying the princely sum of one shilling (worth about £7.50 today) for the privilege.

Sir Walter Scott, instrumental in the Honours' rediscovery, was soon involved in another scheme - the return of Mons Meg to the castle from her 'exile' in the Tower of London. After prolonged lobbying, the Tower authorities were persuaded to part with her and in March 1829 the great medieval bombard arrived by ship at Leith. From there she was escorted to the castle by three troops of cavalry and the 73rd Regiment of Foot.

The momentum increased. In 1836 the so-called 'Queen Mary's Rooms' in the Palace (where King James VI had been born) were vacated by the Army and opened to visitors. In 1846 St Margaret's Chapel [11] was recognised among a clutter of buildings close to where Mons Meg had been positioned. These later structures were swept away and the tiny oratory, the oldest building standing in the castle, was restored much as visitors see it today.

ʼs Meg proudly
'isplay beside
largaret's Chapel
ıt 1860. The great
' gun was moved
ors in 1980 for its
-term preservation.

The climax came in 1891 with the completion of the restoration of the Great Hall [18] by the Edinburgh architect Hippolyte Jean Blanc. His was a rather fanciful scheme and the result is a magnificent Victorian interior, but not at all as it would have appeared in King James IV's day. Blanc was also responsible for the Argyle Tower [13] which William Nelson, the Edinburgh publisher and financier of both restoration schemes, rather hoped might become the new home of the Honours of Scotland. He was to be disappointed.

The new role of the castle as an ancient monument was confirmed in 1905 when the War Office transferred responsibility for all the buildings to the Office of Works. The main garrison finally marched out of the ancient fortress in 1923 to their new home, Redford Barracks, in the suburbs of the city, though the castle still serves as an Army headquarters.

Soldiers from the 92nd Regiment (the Gordon Highlanders) pose with their families at the Forewall Battery in 1846, photographed by David Octavius Hill.
(Courtesy of the Scottish United Services Museum.)

The National Shrine

As the soldiers marched out in 1923 planning had already begun to convert the vacated North Barracks in Crown Square into the national shrine to commemorate the Scottish dead of the Great War. Sir Robert Lorimer, the architect, and his team of artists and craftsmen, completed the work in 1927 and the Scottish National War Memorial [20] was opened by the Prince of Wales (later King Edward VIII) on 14 July of that year.

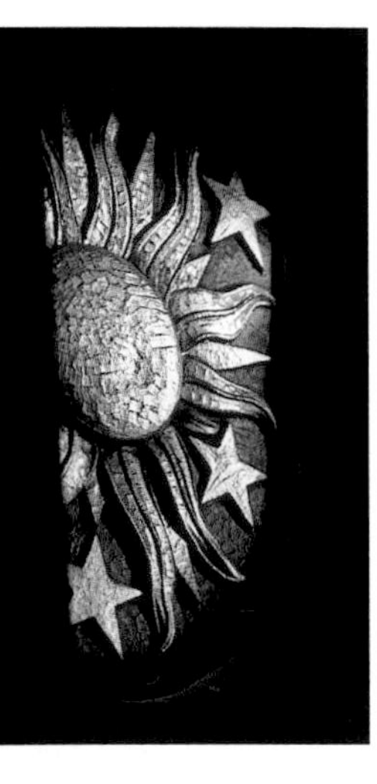

The Duke of Atholl, who chaired the Committee for the War Memorial, also proposed a War Museum and in 1933 the Naval and Military Museum was opened in the Queen Anne Building. That museum continues in the castle today as the Scottish United Services Museum, a department of the National Museums of Scotland. Two regimental museums, those of the Royal Scots and the Royal Scots Dragoon Guards, also have their home in the castle.

The Shrine in the apse and (inset) details from the Scottish National War Memorial.

Troops parade on the Esplanade during the First World War. (Courtesy of the Scottish United Services Museum.)

The 'One O'Clock' Gun

On Mills Mount Battery beside the Cartshed [7] is the signal gun, fired every day (except Sundays, Good Friday and Christmas Day) at 13.00 hours. The citizens of Edinburgh take it for granted and check their watches; visitors jump out of their skin!

The story of the gun begins in 1846. John Hewitt, an Edinburgh businessman, while on a visit to Paris, was astonished to hear a gun fire and to see people refer to their watches. On enquiry he discovered that the gun was fired by the action of the sun's rays on a burning glass. On his return he pressed for something similar in Scotland's capital city, but nothing happened until the time ball was erected on the Nelson Monument on Calton Hill in 1852. He then suggested that this visual signal, designed for the use of ships in the port of Leith, should be accompanied by an audible signal. His idea was taken up and in June 1861 the first firing took place from Edinburgh Castle. It has continued uninterrupted ever since, except for periods during the two World Wars.

The original gun was a 64-pounder muzzle-loader emplaced on the Half-Moon Battery. It took four men to fire. The present gun on the Mills Mount Battery is a Second World War 25-pounder fired by just one man.

The Tattoo

The castle is never more alive than when the Tattoo is taking place on the Esplanade. It began when the city held its first International Festival in the summer of 1947. The Army staged an evening military display on the Esplanade. The march and countermarch of the pipes and drums set against one of the most dramatic backdrops anywhere in the world made it an immediate success and the Tattoo has been repeated ever since. Each Tattoo closes with the appearance of the lone piper on the battlements of the castle.

The Stone of Destiny

On St. Andrew's Day, 1996, Edinburgh Castle became the home of one of Scotland's most powerful symbols – the Stone of Destiny. Until its removal from Scone Abbey to London in 1296, the Stone had served as the seat on which the Scottish Kings had been inaugurated for over 400 years. For nearly 700 years monarchs of England and later rulers of Great Britain and Ireland were crowned on the Stone in Westminster Abbey. Now the Stone rests again in Scotland, in the Crown Room alongside the Honours of Scotland.

We first encountered the castle rock as a mighty volcanic eruption. We leave i 340 million years later as the dominant nationa symbol of Scotland, national shrine, publi spectacle and visitor attraction, and still ar Army headquarters.

For further information about Edinburgl Castle, its story and its treasures, the followin are recommended:

I MacIvor *Edinburgh Castle* (1993)
J Gifford, C McWilliam & D Walker *The Building of Scotland: Edinburgh* (1984)
C Burnett & C Tabraham *The Honours of Scotlana The Story of the Scottish Crown Jewels* (1993)
I Hay *Their Name Liveth: The Book of the Scottisi National War Memorial* (1985)
L Menzies et al *St Margaret Queen of Scotland anc her Chapel* (1985)
D Breeze & G Munro *The Stone of Destiny: Symbo of Nationhood* (1997)
Also available is a 29 minute video *Edinburg Castle: The Official Souvenir Video.*